WILD AGE

CREATURES OF THE SKY

STEVE PARKER

QEB Publishing

Project Editor: Carey Scott
Designer: Stefan Morris Design
Illustrations: The Art Agency and MW Digital Graphics

Picture Researcher: Maria Joannou

Library of Congress Cataloging-in-Publication Data
Parker, Steve, 1952-
   Creatures of the Sky/ Steve Parker.
     p. cm. -- (QEB wild age)
Includes index.
   ISBN 978-1-59566-912-4 (lib. bdg.)
1. Paleontology--Mesozoic--Juvenile literature. 2. Paleontology--Cenozoic--
Juvenile literature. 3. Animals, Fossil--Juvenile literature. I.Title.
   QE731.P37 2011
   560--dc22   2010001151

ISBN 978-1-59566-912-4

Printed in China

Published in the United States
by
QEB Publishing, Inc.
3 Wrigley, Suite A
Irvine, CA 92618

www.qed-publishing.co.uk

Picture credits

Key: t=top, b=bottom, r=right, l=left, c=centre
Alamy Images 19th era 23t, 30bl; **Bridgeman Art Library** Private Collection/©Look and Learn 5cl,
8-9t, 28tr; **Corbis** Jonathan Blair 9b, 28bl, Layne Kennedy 16-17, 29cl (confuciusornis), Colin Keates 27b,
30cl (palaeochiropteryx); **DK Images** Jon Hughes/Bedrock Studios 4cl, 25b, 30cr (titanis), Peter Visscher
4br, Jon Hughes 5bl, 29cl (pterodaustro), Gary Ombler 17br, 29tl; **Getty Images** De Agostini Picture
Library 4cr, 4-5t, 19b, 28tl, 28cl (coelurosauravus), 30cr (teratornis), AFP/Cal Polytech University/Stringer
5tr, Dorling Kindersley 5cr (bat), 26-27, 30cl (icaronycteris); **Istockphoto** Dawn Hagan 3b, Breckeni
5br; **Photolibrary** De Agostini Editore 4bl, 4bl (plant), 4br (tiny land animal), 5cr, 7t, 10, 13r, 24-25, 28cl
(kuehneosaurus), 28cr (anuroghathus), 24-25, 30tr, Oxford Scientific 15tr, 28br, Phototake Science/Carolina
Biological Supply Company 21r, 29tr; **Photoshot** NHPA/Andrea Ferrari 12-13, 29cr (quetzalcoatlus); **Science
Photo Library** Sinclair Stammers 6-7b; **Shutterstock** Jim Barber 2t, Steve Collender 2b, Ryan M. Bolton
3t; **Stock Exchange** 1; **The Art Agency** Robin Boutell 18-19t, 20-21, 22-23b, 30tl, 30br, Robin Carter 5cl
(early bird), 14-15, 28cr (Archeopteryx);
Topham Picturepoint Ullsteinbild 11, 29cr (pteranodon)

All maps: **Mark Walker** MW Digital Graphics

The words in **bold** are
explained in the Glossary
on page 31.

CONTENTS

THE FIRST FLIERS

Today there are thousands of different flying creatures—many kinds of birds, bats at night-time, and flies, butterflies, and other insects. But long ago, the skies were empty.

The first fliers, more than 350 million years ago, were probably tiny insects. They were similar to the dragonflies of today, but much smaller. We know about them from their **fossils**—body parts preserved in the rocks and turned to stone.

The biggest-ever flying insect was **Meganeura** from 300 million years ago. With wings 29.5 inches (75 centimeters) across, it was more than three times larger than today's dragonflies. It swooped down to catch smaller insects on the ground and among plants.

◗ *Meganeura* was the size of today's big birds, such as crows. It had plenty of bugs, worms, and other food in the warm, wet swamps of the Carboniferous Period.

Early winged insects

Giant dragon

360 mya

300 mya

Ediacaran		Cambrian	Ordovician		Silurian		Devonian	Carboniferous	Per
before 542 mya		542–488 mya	488–444 mya		444–416 mya		416–359 mya	359–299 mya	299–25

550 mya   500 mya   400 mya   300 mya

540 mya Shelled sea animals   **460 mya** Land plants **430 mya** Tiny land animals   **360 mya** Four-legged land animals

⬤ This bee is many millions of years old. But it is preserved in a substance called **amber**, like hardened tree sap. We can see every detail of its wings and how it flew.

⬤ Prehistoric time is divided into periods, which have their own names. Each period started and ended a certain number of millions of years ago (mya).

First pterosaurs
220 mya

Early birds
155 mya

Bats appear
55 mya

Biggest-ever birds
6 mya

Triassic 251–200 mya	Jurassic 200–145 mya	Cretaceous 145–65 mya	Paleogene 65–23 mya	Neogene 23–2.6 mya	Quaternary 2.6 mya–now

200 mya   **100 mya**   NOW

230 mya Early dinosaurs

65 mya Mass extinction kills off most land and many sea animals.

GLIDERS AND SWOOPERS

Some "flying" animals, like today's flying squirrels, are not true fliers. They cannot stay in the air for long, but are gliders that gradually swoop downward. Long ago, very different animals did this.

The lizard-like *Coelurosauravus* could glide well on large flaps of skin, one on either side of its body, held out by long thin bones. It probably did this to escape from enemies chasing it through the branches.

An even bigger **reptile** glider was *Kuehneosaurus*. With wing flaps as long as your arms, it drifted slowly downward as though wearing two parachutes.

HOW BIG?

Coelurosauravus
15.8 inches (40 centimeters) long

◗ *Kuehneosaurus* was about 27.6 inches (70 centimeters) long and it lived at the same time as the early dinosaurs. Maybe it was gliding along and one of the meat-eating dinosaurs jumped up to catch and eat it.

◗ *Coelurosauravus* could not flap or beat its wings. But it could alter their shape to steer left or right, with the help of its long tail. These are its preserved fossils from more than 250 million years ago.

WILD FILE

Coelurosauravus

GROUP Reptiles

WHEN Late Permian Period

FOOD Small worms, bugs

FOSSIL SITES Western Europe, Madagascar

● Fossil sites

ON THE WING

To be a true flier, a creature must be able to stay in the air for many minutes, rise up and swoop down, and control where it goes. Could pterosaurs do this?

Yes, they could. **Pterosaurs** lived at the same time as the **dinosaurs**. The first ones could only flap weakly. Gradually they became bigger, better, faster fliers, with powerful wing-beating muscles in their shoulders.

Dimorphodon probably flew over water to grab fish from the surface. It had a beak-like mouth filled with tiny sharp teeth to grip slippery **prey**.

WILD!

A pterosaur's wing was supported by the very long thin bones of its fourth finger. It may have used its other fingers for grabbing prey from the sea's surface or from ledges along the cliffs.

HOW BIG?

Dimorphodon
Wingspan 4.6 feet (1. 4 meters)

The first pterosaurs, such as *Dimorphodon*, had a long trailing tail that probably helped them to turn in the air. These creatures could walk and run on all fours as well as fly.

WILD FILE

Dimorphodon

GROUP Tailed pterosaurs

WHEN Early Jurassic Period

FOOD Fish, insects, perhaps small animals such as lizards

WHERE Europe, North and Central America

● Fossil sites

The fossils of *Eudimorphodon* show it had some long fang-like teeth, probably to bite wriggly victims such as fish. The 100 teeth behind them were smaller but still very sharp.

STRANGE LOOKS

As dinosaurs took over the land, pterosaurs began to rule the skies. They became larger and stronger, and they hunted many kinds of creatures—especially fish.

Some pterosaurs had very strange body parts. Huge **Pteranodon** had a tall flap of bone on its head, called a head **crest**. This probably helped it to steer and balance while flying.

Other pterosaurs had very long, slim beaks that curved up at the end, and were filled with hundreds of thin, bendy teeth, like brush bristles. Perhaps they swished their beaks through the water to catch tiny creatures as food.

⚫ With a body just 3.5 inches (9 centimeters) long, **Anurognathus** may have been the smallest pterosaur. Its large eyes were useful for finding insects, which it snapped up in its tiny, spiky teeth.

WILD FILE

Pteranodon

GROUP Tail-less pterosaurs
WHEN Late Cretaceous Period
FOOD Fish, squid, other creatures
WHERE North America

● Fossil sites

HOW BIG?

Pteranodon
Wingspan up to almost 30 feet (9 meters)

● Later pterosaurs, such as *Pteranodon*, did not have a long tail like the early ones. The head was as big as a grown-up person's. More than 1000 fossils of *Pteranodon* have been found.

BIGGEST-EVER FLIERS

Near the end of the Age of Dinosaurs, pterosaurs became even more massive. Quetzalcoatlus was perhaps the biggest flying creature that ever lived.

Some experts thought that *Quetzalcoatlus* flew low over water to catch fish. Others suggested that it was a **scavenger**, pecking flesh from the dead bodies of dinosaurs and other animals. A newer idea is that *Quetzalcoatlus* walked on all fours, stabbing its victims such as baby dinosaurs.

Quetzalcoatlus and all other pterosaurs died out 65 million years ago, along with dinosaurs and many other kinds of creatures.

HOW BIG?

Quetzalcoatlus
Wingspan 39 feet (12 meters)

WILD!

Quetzalcoatlus could fold its wings back and up, and use its finger claws as front feet. With its back feet as well, it could run along the ground on its feet and claws faster than you can!

● **Ornithocherius** lived in what is now Brazil, South America. Its wings measured 20 feet (6 meters) from tip to tip—as long as a big car.

◑ *Quetzalcoatlus* may have soared over the mountains and plains like an enormous vulture, looking for dead animals to feast on.

WILD FILE

Quetzalcoatlus

GROUP Tail-less pterosaurs

WHEN Late Cretaceous Period

FOOD Medium-sized animals
        such as baby dinosaurs

WHERE North America

● Fossil sites

EARLY BIRDS

In the middle of the Age of the Dinosaurs, some of the small meat-eating dinosaurs changed. They grew feathers, their arms turned to wings, and they became the first birds.

The earliest bird was *Archaeopteryx*. In many ways it was still similar to a small dinosaur. It had teeth in its beak, which no birds have today. It also had bones in its long tail, while modern birds have just feathers. *Archaeopteryx* also had finger claws on its wings, unlike today's birds.

Archaeopteryx was probably a good runner as well as a flier, and it may have hunted food on the ground.

WILD FILE

Archaeopteryx

GROUP Toothed birds

WHEN Late Jurassic Period

FOOD Insects and small animals such as lizards

WHERE Europe

● Fossil sites

WILD!

Like all fossils, the fossil feathers of *Archaeopteryx* have no traces of their original colors. So people who make pictures of this bird can color it any way they like!

● Take away the big, long feathers of *Archaeopteryx* and it would look very similar to a little dinosaur with small feathers, like this *Protarchaeopteryx*.

◑ *Archaeopteryx* spreads its wings, ready for takeoff. It was probably not an expert flier, like modern birds, but it could swoop and glide quite well.

HOW BIG?

Archaeopteryx
Wingspan 23.6 inches (60 centimeters)

BIRDS TAKE OFF

Toward the end of the Age of Dinosaurs, many new kinds of birds appeared in the skies. Some were as small as sparrows, while others were much larger—even bigger than us.

Confuciusornis was one of the bigger birds of the time, about the size of today's crow. Its many fossils show that *Confuciusornis* formed big groups or flocks that probably fed and rested together.

Eoalulavis was much smaller, hardly the size of a sparrow. Its wing shape was suited to very controlled flying, especially when taking off or landing. Birds were truly becoming expert fliers.

❶ *Confuciusornis* fossils come from China and are about 120 million years old. This was the first bird to have a proper beak, rather than dinosaur-like jaws and teeth.

WILD FILE

Confuciusornis

GROUP Birds
WHEN Early Cretaceous Period
FOOD Seeds, perhaps small animals
WHERE China

● Fossil sites

HOW BIG?

Confuciusornis
Wingpsan 35.4 inches (90 centimeters)

⬤ **Caudipteryx** was about as big as a peacock. It had long feathers on its arms and tail. Yet it was not a bird—it was a dinosaur. Its wings were far too small and weak for flight.

WINGS OVER WATER

The first birds probably fed on the ground or in tree branches. Then some kinds started to feed in water, catching fish and other prey. They became swimmers as well as fliers.

Dasornis was a type of goose, but far bigger than any geese today. It could probably land on water and swim along by kicking with its feet.

When *Dasornis* was hungry, it took off and swooped over the surface to catch slippery fish. It grabbed them using the rows of tiny teeth in its massive beak.

CLOSE COUSINS

Experts are not sure what kind of bird *Dasornis* was. It was probably related to ducks, geese, and swans. Or it could have been a cousin of today's pelicans, or even a member of the stork group.

HOW BIG?

Dasornis
Wingspan 16.4 feet (5 meters)

◗ *Dasornis* had very long, thin wings, like an albatross. This shape is good for gliding long distances without making much effort.

WILD FILE

Dasornis

GROUP Wildfowl birds

WHEN Early Paleogene Period

FOOD Fish, squid, other sea creatures

WHERE Europe

● Fossil sItes

◗ *Presbyornis* was a tall shorebird with long legs, about 3 feet (1 meter) high. It lived after the Age of the Dinosaurs, around 40–60 million years ago, in North America.

TO FLY OR NOT?

Today, most birds are expert fliers. But some, such as ostriches and penguins, cannot fly at all. Long ago there were also flightless birds.

Hesperornis was a seabird that lost the power of flight and turned into an expert swimmer. Its wings were tiny, but its legs had big paddle-shaped feet for moving very fast through the water. *Hesperornis* chased fish and similar food under the surface.

Like *Hesperornis*, **Ichthyornis** had teeth in its beak and probably ate fish. But it caught them while flying, by swooping down to just under the water's surface, then taking off again.

HOW BIG?

Hesperornis
6.5 feet (2 meters) high

WILD!

When *Hesperornis* fossils were first discovered over a hundred years ago, experts thought they were the remains of a fierce lizard that swam in the sea!

Hesperornis

GROUP Seabirds

WHEN Late Cretaceous Period

FOOD Fish, other water creatures

WHERE North America, including Canada

Fossil sites

Ichthyornis was the Dinosaur Age version of our modern seagulls and terns. It was about gull-sized and its fossils suggest it had strong wings and flying muscles.

Hesperornis was a big, heavy bird that could only waddle on land. It may have been hunted by hungry dinosaurs prowling along the shore.

BIG COUSINS

Long ago, the birds that flew in the skies were close relatives of birds alive today. Some of those distant relations were giants!

The largest-ever eagle was *Harpagornis*, or Haast's eagle, from New Zealand. Its prey included the flightless birds known as **moas**. Both the eagle and the moas died out—but only about 1400 years ago.

The biggest penguin today is the emperor penguin, at 47 inches (120 centimeters) tall. About 40 million years ago, the giant penguin ***Anthropornis*** was 15.8 inches (40 centimeters) taller—as high as an adult person!

WILD!

Harpagornis lived at the same time as early people. It was such a strong and powerful animal that *Harpagornis* may have even carried away human babies and young children.

HOW BIG?

Harpagornis
Wingspan 10.5 feet (3.2 meters)

◗ The giant penguin *Anthropornis* lived about 40 million years ago. It probably hunted fish and squid in the sea and rested on land, like today's penguins.

◗ *Harpargonis* swooped down to carry off its prey, mostly newborn and young flightless birds. It had huge claws, or talons, to stab into its victims, and a sharp hooked beak to tear their flesh apart.

WILD FILE

Harpagornis

GROUP Birds of prey

WHEN Until 1400 years ago

FOOD Large birds and ground animals

WHERE New Zealand

New Zealand

● Fossil sites

SHADOWS IN THE SKY

Giant birds of prey once cast a shadow over the land. There were also fearsome hunting birds that could not fly—but they could outrun most other animals.

Argentavis was the biggest flying bird of all time. Its wings were twice as long as the albatross, the bird with the longest wings now. Its sharp beak shows that it probably scavenged, eating dying or dead creatures.

Titanis was flightless, like today's ostrich, but much stronger and heavier. It ran after victims on its powerful legs, and tore them apart with its fierce hooked beak.

WILD!

Argentavis was so big and heavy that, to take off, it probably jumped from a cliff or ran downhill into the wind. Once in the air, it could glide for hours without flapping its huge wings.

HOW BIG?

Argentavis
Wingspan 23 feet (7 meters)

◑ We don't know if *Argentavis* had a bare head and neck, like today's vultures. If so, it would not have had feathers to get covered in blood as it pecked inside dead animals.

◐ *Titanis* was as tall as a doorway. This top predator could even catch and tear apart the small horses that lived in the Neogene Period.

NIGHT FLIERS

As birds took over the skies during the daytime, other creatures began to hunt in the dark. They were furry mammals whose arms became long wings—the bats.

The first known **bat** was *Icaronycteris*, from 50–40 million years ago. It looked very similar to bats of today, with wings of leathery skin held out by long finger bones.

Icaronycteris found its way in the dark like today's bats. It made squeaks and listened to the echoes bouncing back off nearby objects. We know this from the small, delicate fossils of its ear and mouth bones.

HOW BIG?

Icaronycteris
Wingspan 13.8-15.8 inches
(35–40 centimeters)

◗ *Icaronycteris* caught small flying creatures, such as moths and flies, with its sharp teeth. It could hang upside down by its feet, just like modern bats.

Icaronycteris

GROUP Bats (mammals)

WHEN Early–Mid Paleogene Period

FOOD Moths, similar flying insects

WHERE North America

● Fossil sites

◐ Fossils of the bat *Palaeochiropteryx* come from Germany. They look very jumbled here, but the long arm bones and thin finger bones can be seen.

CLOSE COUSINS

Bats did not develop, or **evolve**, from feathery birds. They probably evolved from small, furry tree-living **mammals**, which were similar to today's tree-shrews.

WILD GUIDE

Meganeura

Pronunciation
meg-ah-nure-ah

Meaning Big nerves or nets

Group Insects

Time Carboniferous, 300 mya

Wingspan 29.5 in (75 cm)

Length 35.4 in (90 cm)

Dimorphodon

Pronunciation
die-mor-foe-don

Meaning Two forms of teeth

Group Tailed pterosaurs

Time Early Jurassic, 190 mya

Wingspan 55.1 (140 cm)

Length 39.4 in (100 cm)

Coelurosauravus

Pronunciation
seel-ure-oh-saw-rave-us

Meaning Hollow reptile bird

Group Reptiles

Time Late Permian, 255 mya

Wingspan 11.8 in (30 cm)

Length 15.8 in (40 cm)

Archaeopteryx

Pronunciation
ark-ee-op-tur-ix

Meaning Ancient wing

Group Toothed birds

Time Late Jurassic, 150 mya

Wingspan 23.6 in (60 cm)

Length 20 in (50 cm)

Kuehneosaurus

Pronunciation
koo-enn-ee-oh-saw-rus

Meaning Kuehn's lizard

Group Reptiles

Time Late Triassic, 200 mya

Wingspan 15.8 in (40 cm)

Length 27.6 in (70 cm)

Anurognathus

Pronunciation
ann-your-og-nay-thus

Meaning Without tail jaw

Group Tailed pterosaurs

Time Late Jurassic, 150 mya

Wingspan 20 in (50 cm)

Length 3.5 in (9 cm)

Eudimorphodon

Pronunciation
you-dee-mor-foe-don

Meaning Truly two forms of teeth

Group Tailed pterosaurs

Time Late Triassic, 205 mya

Wingspan 39.4 in (100 cm)

Length 39.4 in (100 cm)

Protarchaeopteryx

Pronunciation
prowt-ark-ee-op-tur-ix

Meaning Before Archaeopteryx

Group Dinosaurs

Time Early Cretaceous, 125 mya

Weight 8.8 lbs (4 kg)

Length 3.3 ft (1 m)

WILD GUIDE

Caudipteryx

Pronunciation cord-ip-tur-ix

Meaning Tail feather

Group Dinosaurs

Time Early Cretaceous, 125 mya

Weight 6.6 lbs (3 kg)

Length 3.3 ft (1 m)

Ichthyornis

Pronunciation ick-thee-or-niss

Meaning Fish bird

Group Prehistoric seabirds

Time Late Cretaceous, 90–75 mya

Wingspan 23.6 in (60 cm)

Length 11.8 in (30 cm)

Confuciusornis

Pronunciation con-few-she-us-orn-iss

Meaning Confucius bird

Group Beaked birds

Time Early Cretaceous, 120 mya

Wingspan 35.4 in (90 cm)

Length 11.8 in (30 cm)

Pteranodon

Pronunciation tear-an-oh-don

Meaning Toothless wing

Group Tail-less pterosaurs

Time Late Cretaceous, 70 mya

Wingspan Up to 29.5 ft (9 m)

Length 6.5 ft (2 m)

Pterodaustro

Pronunciation tear-oh-daow-strow

Meaning South wind wing

Group Tail-less pterosaurs

Time Mid-Cretaceous, 105 mya

Wingspan 8.2 ft (2.5 m)

Length 3.3 ft (1 m)

Quetzalcoatlus

Pronunciation kwet-zal-coe-at-lus

Meaning After the Aztec god Quetzalcoatl

Group Tail-less pterosaurs

Time Late Cretaceous, 70 mya

Wingspan 39 ft (12 m)

Length 20 ft (6 m)

Ornithocheirus

Pronunciation or-nith-oh-kie-rus

Meaning Bird hand

Group Tail-less pterosaurs

Time Late Cretaceous, 95 mya

Wingspan 20 ft (6 m)

Length 6.5 ft (2 m)

Presbyornis

Pronunciation press-bee-orn-iss

Meaning Elder bird

Group Waterbirds

Time Early Palaeogene, 55 mya

Wingspan 6.5 ft (2 m)

Height 3.3 ft (1 m)

WILD GUIDE

Dasornis

Pronunciation
das-orn-iss

Meaning Hairy bird

Group Modern birds

Time Early Paleogene, 50 mya

Wingspan 16.4 ft (5 m)

Length 3.3 ft (1 m)

Icaronycteris

Pronunciation
ik-are-oh-nick-tur-iss

Meaning Icarus night creature

Group Bats

Time Early-Mid Paleogene,
50–40 mya

Wingspan 13.8-15.8 in (35–40 cm)

Length 6 in (15 cm)

Palaeochiropteryx

Pronunciation
pale-ee-owe-kye-rop-tur-ix

Meaning Ancient hand wing

Group Bats

Time Mid Palaeogene, 47 mya

Wingspan 9.8 in (25 cm)

Length 3.9 in (10 cm)

Anthropornis

Pronunciation
an-throw-poor-nis

Meaning Human-like bird

Group Penguins

Time Mid Palaeogene, 40 mya

Wingspan 3.6 ft (1.1 m)

Height 5.3 ft (1.6 m)

Argentavis

Pronunciation
are-jen-tay-viss

Meaning Magnificent
Argentine bird

Group Birds of prey

Time Late Neogene, 5 mya

Wingspan 23 ft (7 m)

Length 11.5 ft (3.5 m)

Titanis

Pronunciation
tie-tan-iss

Meaning Titanic

Group Flightless birds

Time Late Neogene
and Quaternary, 5–2 mya

Height 8.2 ft (2.5 m)

Weight 330 lbs (150 kg)

Teratornis

Pronunciation
terra-torn-iss

Meaning Monster bird

Group Birds of prey

Time Quaternary, until 10,000 ya

Wingspan 11.8 ft (3.6 m)

Height 29.5 in (75 cm)

Harpagornis

Pronunciation
harp-ah-gorn-iss

Meaning Hook-beaked bird

Group Birds of prey

Time Quaternary, until 1400 ya

Wingspan 10.5 ft (3.2 m)

Length 3.9 ft (1.2 m)

GLOSSARY

Amber Resin, a sticky liquid made by certain kinds of plants, which has gone hard over millions of years.

Anurognathus A small pterosaur, with wings about 15.8 inches (40 centimeters) across, which lived 150 million years ago.

Anthropornis A huge penguin, tall as an adult person, that lived 40 million years ago.

Bats Mammals with front limbs or arms shaped like wings, which can fly very well even in darkness.

Birds of prey Birds that hunt other creatures for food. Most have a sharp, hooked beak and long pointed claws called talons.

Caudipteryx A small dinosaur covered with bird-like feathers that lived about 125 million years ago.

Crest Bone on the top of the head.

Dasornis A huge seabird with wings 16.5 feet (5 meters) across, probably a relative of today's geese and swans, that lived about 50 million years ago.

Dimorphodon An early kind of pterosaur from almost 200 million years ago, with wings 55 inches (140 centimeters) across and a long, trailing tail.

Dinosaurs Types of reptile that lived millions of years ago. All dinosaurs are now extinct.

Evolve When living things change gradually over a long period of time.

Fossil Any part of a plant or animal that has been preserved in rock. Also traces of plants or animals, such as footprints.

Flying animals Creatures that can stay in the air for more than a couple of minutes, and control their flight so that they climb, dive, and steer where they want to go.

Icaronycteris One of the first bats, from almost 50 million years ago, with wings up to 15.8 inches (40 centimeters) across.

Ichthyornis A gull-like seabird from about 90–75 million years ago, with wings 20-23.6 inches (50–60 centimeters) from tip to tip.

Mammal An animal that has hair or fur and produces milk for its babies.

Meganeura A giant dragonfly-type insect with wings 29.5 inches (75 centimeters) across that lived 300 million years ago.

Moas Huge birds that could not fly and once lived on the islands of New Zealand. There were about five or six kinds, some up to 11.5 feet (3.5 meters) tall. They have all died out.

Ornithocheirus A very big pterosaur that lived almost 100 million years ago in South America, with wings up to 20 feet (6 meters) across.

Pteranodon One of the largest pterosaurs. There were many kinds, some with wings more than 26 feet (8 meters) from tip to tip.

Pterosaurs Flying cousins of dinosaurs that lived at the same time, from about 225 to 65 million years ago. They had furry bodies and front limbs shaped like wings.

Presbyornis A tall wading bird that walked along the seashore and shallows around 40–60 million years ago.

Prey A creature that is killed and eaten by another animal, the predator.

Reptile A scaly, usually cold-blooded animal, such as a lizard, snake, crocodile, turtle, or dinosaur. Some reptiles had hair, and others, such as some dinosaurs, had feathers.

Scavengers Animals that feed on dead bodies killed by other creatures, rather than killing them themselves.

INDEX